Colouring Books

FOR Kids

Awesome Animals

Published in 2018 by The Future Teacher Foundation

© The Future Teacher Foundation 2018

www.thefutureteacherfoundation.com

ISBN-13: 978-1717276483

ISBN-10: 1717276482

For printing and manufacturing information please see the last page.

All images copyright © The Future Teacher Foundation 2018

If you choose to remove pages for framing, ask an adult to carefully extract with a scalpel and ruler.

Warning: This book is not suitable for children under 36 months of age due to potential small parts - choking hazard.

This Book Belongs To

_____

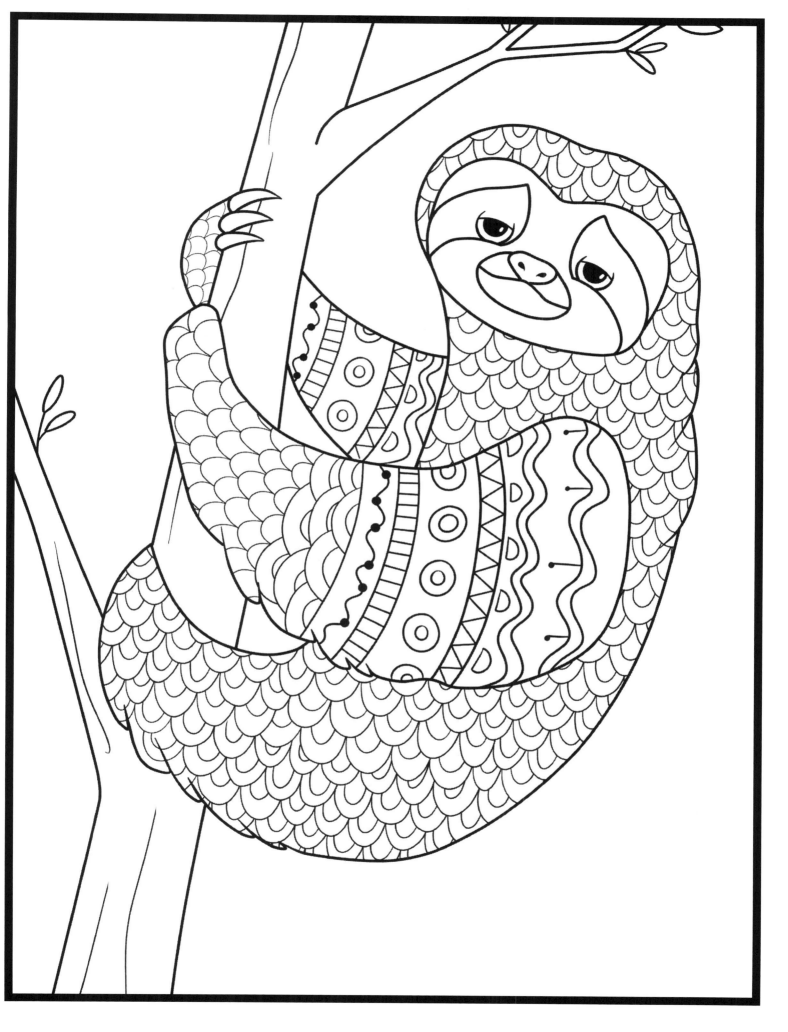

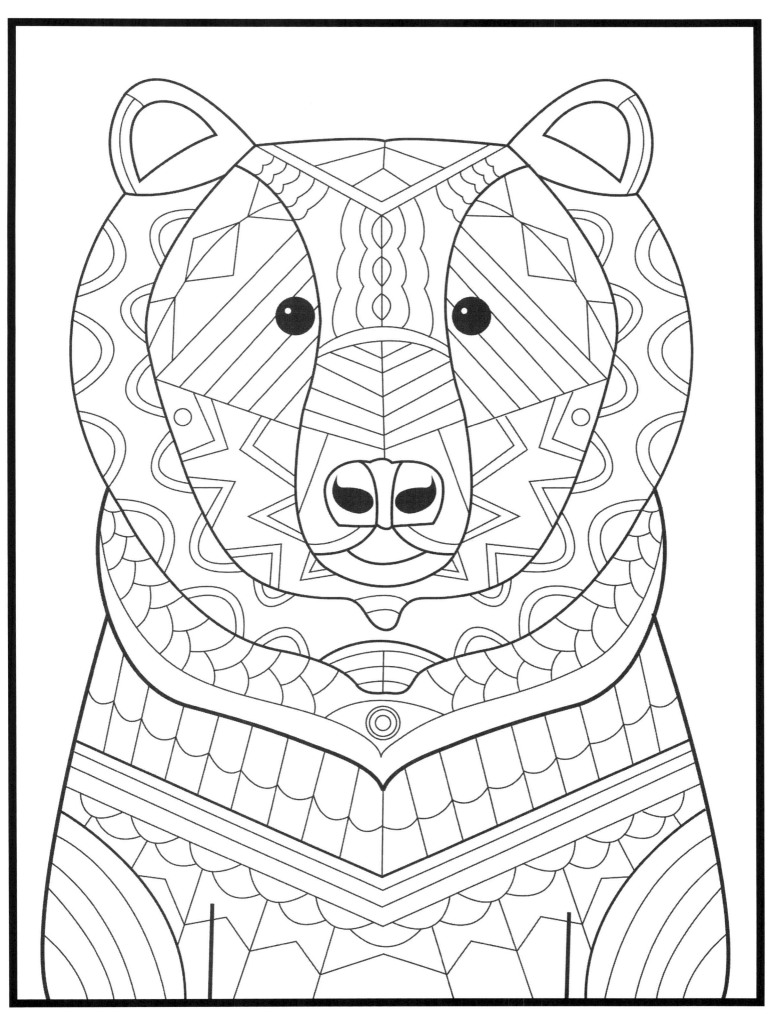

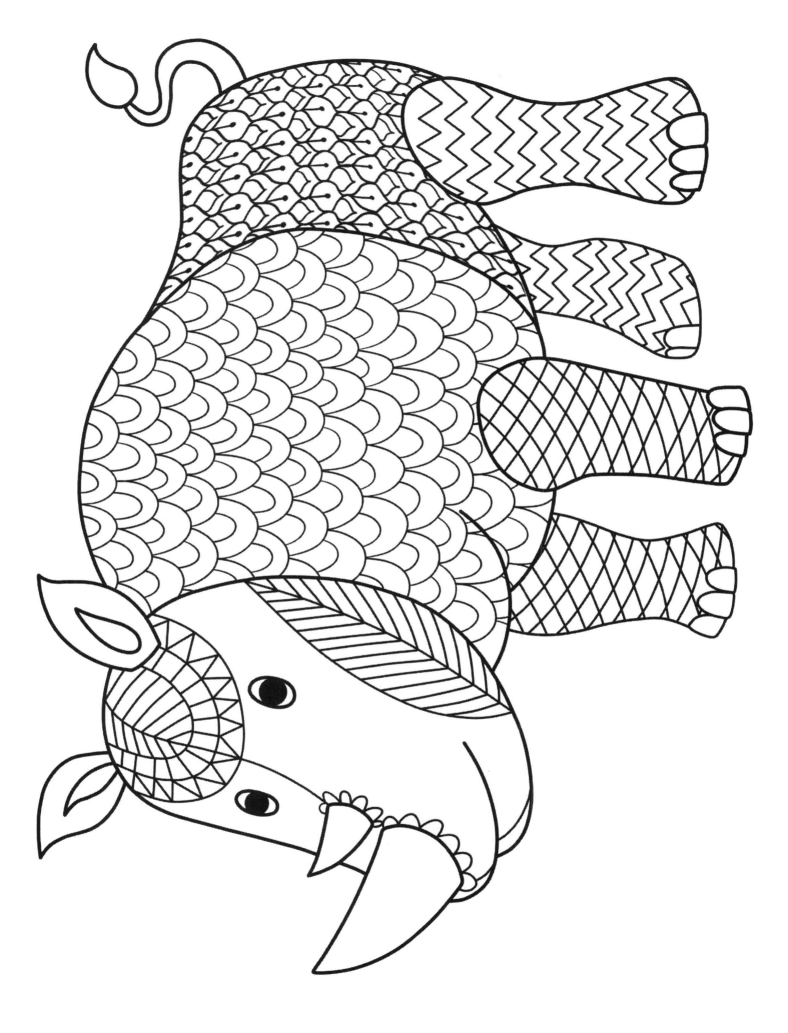

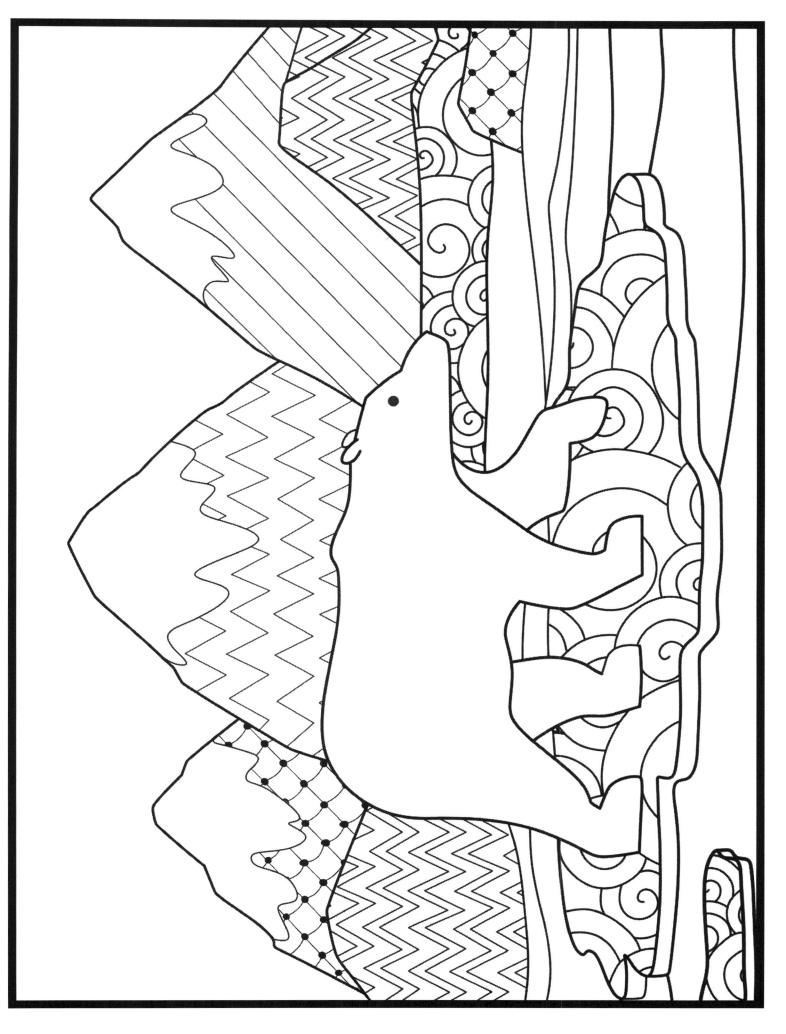

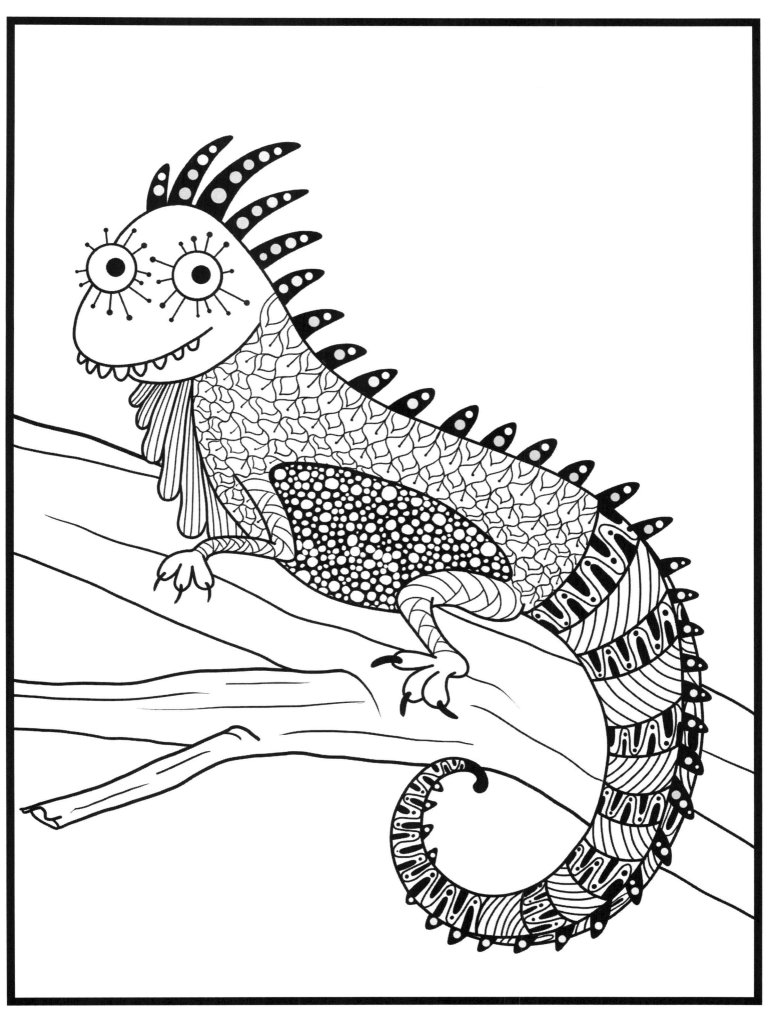

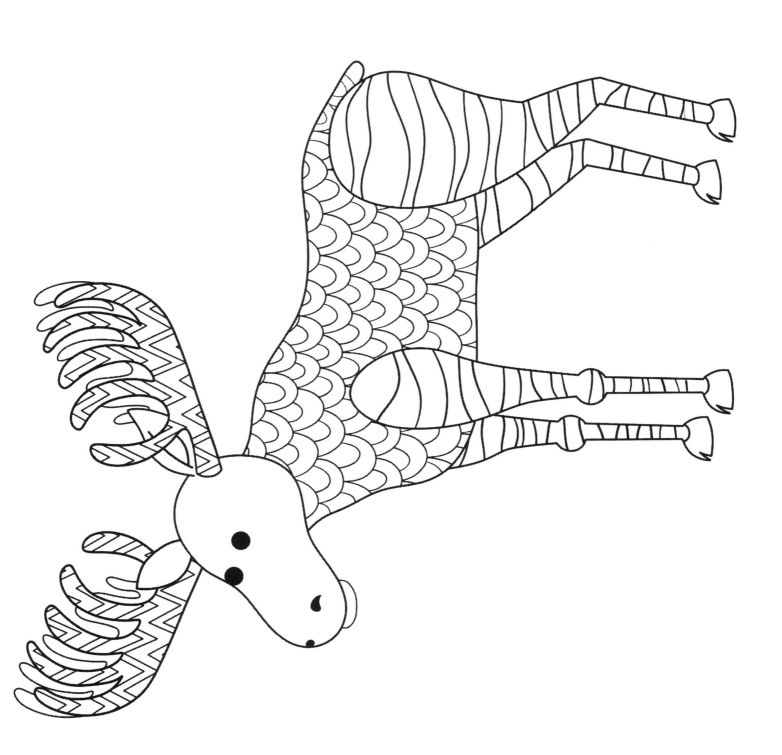

Printed in Poland
by Amazon Fulfillment
Poland Sp. z o.o., Wrocław